Ben of the Island:
The Iceboats and the Phantom Ship

Written By: Terrilyn Kerr
Illustrated by: Nancy Perkins

Copyright 2020 by Terrilyn Kerr. Illustrations created by Nancy Perkins All rights reserved. No part of this book may be used in any form or by any means graphical, electronic, or mechanical" without written permission of the copyright owner.

ISBN: 978-1-987852-26-4

First printing May 2020

Author: Terrilyn Kerr; terrilynkerr@gmail.com

Illustrator: Nancy Perkins; nancyperkinspainter@hotmail.com

Publisher: Wood Island Prints; 670 Trans-Canada Highway, Route 1; Wood Islands, PE C0A 1R0; (902) 962-3335; schultz@pei.sympatico.ca; www.woodislandsprints.com

This is Terrilyn Kerr`s fourth published children`s book. She lives on Prince Edward Island and writes short stories and poetry besides teaching traditional rug braiding. Terrilyn is inspired daily by the wildlife and sounds of the ocean as she walks the beaches of her beautiful Island home.

Nancy Perkins for many decades has been a painter of mainly nautical themes, working in oils and acrylics. Her work is in Island galleries, private collections and is included in the PEI Provincial Art Bank. She too lives on Prince Edward Island and has collaborated with Terrilyn on two other books.

Dedication

This book is dedicated to all animal companions
who share their lives and love with us every day. Thank you.

The story takes historical facts and blends them with fictional
characters. In both cases, the iceboat crews and
their rescuers were true heroes.

Thank you to Nancy Perkins for her skills
and perseverance as the illustrator.

A thank you as well to my husband Sandy—for his love and
support—and to our family who are always sending
their love and encouragement.

Ben was now five years old. The years had gone by very quickly and he had matured into a large, strong dog with the beautiful copper colouring of the Chesapeake[1] breed. In Wood Islands, he was well known as the lighthouse keeper`s pet and loved because of his courage and wonderful disposition. Ben had already become famous after rescuing a small girl who had wandered away from her home, and by standing his ground against a large black bear, which allowed the lighthouse keeper and his horses to escape to safety.

Ben kept the family cow, horses, goats and chickens safe from the local predators as he made his rounds every day and night, always on the lookout for danger. He was also very playful with these animals and they came to look forward to the times he romped with them. This group had expanded with the recent addition of a donkey which Ben would frequently pretend to attack. The donkey would then bray and race away only to suddenly turn and go after Ben who would howl and run in the other direction! Ben loved the outdoors and his thick, shiny coat kept him warm in the winter and shed the water as he swam in the Northumberland Strait[2] during the summer months.

During the winter months, Ben`s favourite pastime was watching the iceboats.[3] These boats were used to ferry passengers and mail across the Northumberland Strait to Nova Scotia. The eastern route for the iceboats passed between Wood Islands, Prince Edward Island and Caribou, Nova Scotia. The boats would also stop enroute at Pictou Island to pick up and deliver mail to the residents living there.

Ben would watch the crews and passengers as they set out on their journey to Nova Scotia, crews hauling on the attached ropes and passengers either helping or huddled down in the boats. The mornings were frosty and the crews would strain as they pulled the boats across the ice. Ben barked encouragement as they set off, frequently going out onto the ice with them until he turned and headed for home.

Crossing the Strait in the winter was always a dangerous time for both passengers and crews. Sometimes they would get mired in the heavy slush that would pool in areas of open water, and often one or two of the crew would fall through the ice when it didn`t support the weight of the boat. The winds and tides also presented a danger as boats were prone to rapid drifting as a result of these forces.

One day in late January 1885[4] the weather became bitterly cold. The iceboats were due back from Nova Scotia that afternoon and the lighthouse keeper stood on the shore scanning the icy Strait, looking for any sign of them. There was a storm coming and visibility was becoming poor. Still, there was no sign of the boats, crews and passengers, and Ben could smell nothing as he put his nose in the air, trying to catch the scent of the boats and their occupants. The wind was freshening from the Northeast and the boats were in danger of becoming lost in the driving snow.

As the storm raged that night and all the next day, the people at Wood Islands knew that the crews and passengers were indeed lost. The only hope was that they had tipped the boats over onto the ice and were able to huddle underneath them. Even then the cold and wind could cause them great suffering and perhaps even death.

The next day, after the storm abated, a search party was organized. No one knew in which direction to search; the boats could be anywhere along the shore or still out in the middle of the Strait. It was decided that Ben would be sent out towards the east, leading a band of rescuers. He led the men along the shore as they looked, listened and called, hoping to come across the boats. For a whole day they traveled and searched. Then, with sinking spirits, the search party returned to the lighthouse as night fell. They were chilled to the bone and could only imagine just how cold and frightened the people in the iceboats must be. The lighthouse keeper`s wife fed everyone hot soup and fresh bread, and they all found a place to sleep in the lighthouse for the night.

Before dawn the next day, the searchers went out again. This time they headed west, trudging along the shore. Again, Ben led the group but could still smell nothing. It was mid-afternoon and the light was fading when suddenly Ben caught a scent of something new. It was faint but he began to bark and race along the shore. The searchers shouted and ran after Ben as he searched along the ice.

They found the first person on the shore, so cold that he could barely move. While the rescue party looked after the man, Ben kept going. He continued to look for and find weakened crewmembers and passengers along the frozen beaches and out on the ice. It took some time for the rescuers to get to the passengers and crews, and place them on sleds to be dragged to safety.

At last, Ben found the final crewmember lying in a swampy area, too cold and tired to move. Ben realized that the man was close to death so he curled his body around him, lending him some warmth. Ben continued to bark until the rescuers could finally reach them. When they arrived, Ben`s coat was covered in ice and he had a hard time trying to stand. The rescuers placed Ben on a sled with the final survivor, and pulled them both to the horse drawn wagon that was waiting on the other side of the swamp. They made their way to the lighthouse where Ben was laid in front of the fire to get warm. When he couldn`t stop shivering, the lighthouse keeper`s wife wrapped him in a blanket and cuddled him beside the fire.

All the passengers and crewmembers were saved that day. It had been a close call for all of them, and although some of them had severe frostbite, they were all grateful to be alive. Ben had once again proved his worth as a courageous dog, but it took him a long time to recover and feel strong again after that ordeal.

As the winter of 1885 wore on, Ben stayed close to his home and only ventured out with the lighthouse keeper when the livestock needed tending in the barn. That winter was a long, dark one that seemed to go on forever.

    Finally, spring began to peek through the snow and Ben was excited to get outdoors and tease the goats. He would run and chase them, and they would try to butt him with their heads. Once, he got too close to the biggest goat and was knocked head over heels when the goat hit him hard on his side. After that, Ben kept his distance from those grumpy animals.

At last it was warm enough for Ben to take his first swim of the season in the Northumberland Strait. He swam back and forth along the shore, sometimes encountering seals sunning themselves on the rocks.

As he swam, porpoises would occasionally join him, swimming all around him and jumping over him as they frolicked in the water. He also heard the whales spouting from their blowholes farther out in the Strait. These were the times that Ben loved best of all.

When summer finally arrived and the weather turned hot, Ben would stay down by the shore, cooling himself in the salty waters of the Strait. There were often bathers on the beach, frolicking in the waves. Ben would play with them, chasing the sticks that they threw for him.

One day as Ben was bothering the rock crabs along the shore, he heard a shout from one of the bathers. He looked up and saw a man pointing out to sea. He turned his gaze towards the direction the bather was pointing and saw a sailing ship on fire out in the Strait!

The people on shore raised the alarm at the lighthouse. The lighthouse keeper quickly organized the rescuers who then headed out in their boats to save the people on board the burning ship. Ben was a strong swimmer so he was told to get in the boat with the rescuers. It was a terrible sight to see the sails and masts of the schooner on fire. The men rowed as hard as they could to reach the people on board before the ship sank. Most people in those days didn`t know how to swim, so it was critical to reach the boat in time to save the passengers and crew.

As the boats approached the burning ship, Ben and the rescuers were shocked to see the blazing ship disappear! They searched and searched for survivors. Ben jumped into the water and swam towards the spot where he had last seen the ship. Nothing was found ... no flames, no floating timber and no people. There was nothing to be seen anywhere in the surrounding water! Ben was hauled back into one of the boats and the puzzled rescuers rowed back to shore.

It turned out that quite a few witnesses had seen the burning ship. However, no one could explain why the ship had disappeared so suddenly when the rescuers had come close.

As the local people talked about the phenomenon, others told of similar sightings all around the Island. They called the sightings the Phantom Ship or Burning ship.[5] Ben heard that the earliest documented sighting had happened way back in 1786 off Sea Cow Pond. It was certainly a great mystery to everyone, and Ben often wondered what had happened to that ship and why it had disappeared.

Late in the fall, Ben lay by the wood stove, reflecting on all the adventures he had experienced that past year... playing with his friends, the iceboats and the phantom ship. Life was simple but there were also many mysteries he couldn`t explain, and sometimes he wished more things made sense to him.

He had his job looking after the livestock; he knew how to look cute so he would get an extra treat; he knew he was loved and looked after, and perhaps that was all that mattered. Ben sighed contentedly and began to focus on his next meal. He then fell asleep dreaming of chasing rabbits, playing with his friend the donkey, and wondering what new adventures he would have in the coming years.

Endnotes: WIKIPEDIA and P.E.I ARCHIVAL FACTS

1 Chesapeake Bay Retriever: a large-sized breed of dog belonging to the Retriever, Gun dog, and Sporting breed groups. Members of the breed may also be referred to as a Chessie, CBR, or Chesapeake. The breed was developed in the United States Chesapeake Bay area during the 19th century. Historically used by area market hunters to retrieve waterfowl, it is primarily a family pet and hunting companion. They are often known for their love of water and their ability to hunt. It is a medium to large sized dog similar in appearance to the Labrador Retriever. The Chesapeake has a wavy coat, rather than the Labrador`s smooth coat. They are described as having a bright and happy disposition, courage, willingness to work, alertness, intelligence, and love of water as some of their characteristics.

2 Northumberland Strait (French: Detroit de Northumberland): a strait in the southern part of the Gulf of Saint Lawrence in eastern Canada formed by Prince Edward Island and the gulf's eastern, southern and western shores.

3 Northumberland Strait iceboats: A Northumberland Strait iceboat was a rowing boat, typically 5 metres in length, 2 metres in beam, with runners fastened to the hull for dragging over sea ice. Constructed of wood, similar to fishing dories built in Atlantic Canada and New England, the iceboats were operated in the Northumberland Strait during the 19th century and early 20th century, running between Prince Edward Island and the mainland provinces of New Brunswick and Nova Scotia during the winter months between December and April when sea ice made passage by non-icebreaking steam ships impossible. They were also used during the winter months to connect Pictou Island with mainland Nova Scotia, sometimes in conjunction with passages from Prince Edward Island.

The greatest danger that iceboat crews and passengers faced was not the stretches of open water, nor the sea ice, but rather the heavy "slush" that would pool in areas of open water that were in the process of solidifying into ice. There are several accounts of boats becoming mired in these conditions and oars being broken during attempts to row through the slush. Wind and tide formed another danger as the fields of sea ice were prone to rapid drifting because of these forces. There have been accounts of iceboats being swept up or down the Northumberland Strait and landing far from their intended destinations. Stranding also occurred in which case iceboat occupants would huddle on the surface of an ice floe beneath the upended iceboat waiting for storms to pass, sometimes breaking parts of the boat off for firewood to stave off the cold. Not many lives were lost during these perilous crossings.

The two primary routes for iceboats were between Wood Islands, Prince Edward Island

and Caribou, Nova Scotia, (sometimes combined with a stop at Pictou Island, Nova Scotia), and across the Abegweit Passage between Cape Traverse, Prince Edward Island and Cape Jourimain, New Brunswick. This latter route was known as the "Capes Route" and was the longest running iceboat service, operating from December 19, 1827 until 1917 when the icebreaking railcar ferry Prince Edward Island began service on this route.

4 In 1885 three iceboats were lost for two days, and their crews and passengers almost died. Crew and Passengers Involved in the 1885 Incident:

Boat One: In command of Captain Muncey Irving; Crew: Alex (Sandy) Stewart, Blucher Robinson, William Howatt, William Campbell.

Boat Two: In command of Captain Newton Muttart; Crew: Hector Campbell, Mont Campbell, Eph Bell, James A. Howatt.

Boat Three: In command of Captain Hanford Allen; Crew: George Allen, John Allen, Edward Trenholm, Daniel McGlashen.

The passengers were Dr. Peter A. McIntyre, M.P. from Souris, James A. Fraser and Aaron Wilson from Summerside, Albert Glydon of Tignish, Philip Farrell of Sturgeon.

5 Phantom Ship Of The Northumberland Strait: In Canadian ghost lore, the Ghost Ship of Northumberland Strait is a ghost ship said to sail ablaze within the Northumberland Strait, the body of water that separates Prince Edward Island from Nova Scotia and New Brunswick in eastern Canada. The legend of a ghost ship in Northumberland Strait dates back at least 200 years, and it is typically described as a beautiful schooner that has three or four masts with pure white sails, all of which are said to become completely engulfed in flames as onlookers watch. The Northumberland Strait separates Prince Edward Island from New Brunswick and Nova Scotia, and according to local folklore, the ghost ship appears before a northeast wind, and is a forewarning of a storm. A number of legends and ghost stories exist that describe sightings of the ghost ship over the years and include descriptions of distinctive outlines of the ship`s masts and phantom crew members climbing them before the vessel supposedly either completely burns, sinks or vanishes. According to legend, in 1900, a group of sailors boarded a small rowboat in Charlottetown Harbour and raced toward the phantom ship to rescue the crew only to have the ship vanish. In January 2008, 17-year-old Mathieu Giguere told a local newspaper he believed he saw the legendary phantom ship in the Tatamagouche Bay, describing it as a "bright" white and gold ship". Tatamagouche Mountain resident Melvin Langille also claims he saw the ship one night in October, explaining, "I believe in all that stuff and I don`t know what else it would be."